The Prophetic Equation

Thirty Prophets. One Christ. Zero Coincidence.

Christian A. Dickinson

Title: *The Prophetic Equation*
Subtitle: *Thirty Prophets. One Christ. Zero Coincidence.*
Written by: Christian A. Dickinson
Illustrations by: Learning Engineered LLC
Published by: Learning Engineered Publishing

Library of Congress Control Number: 2025938565
ISBN (Print): 978-1-965741-19-1

First Edition: 2025

Printed & Created in: United States of America
Text and Illustration Copyright © 2025

Learning Engineered Publishing is a division of Learning Engineered LLC and a subsidiary of Carpe Diem Unlimited Holdings, Inc.

LEARNING ENGINEERED
PUBLISHING

Dedication

To my daughter, Abigayle Faith Dickinson, whose keen logic and sweetness, shining from Christ within her, reflect the divine design pointing to Jesus.

Contents

Author's Note

My foundation wasn't built in classrooms or formed solely through books. It was forged by watching my dad live his faith—day in, day out—in real life.

Faith wasn't just words for him. It was action, even when no one saw. Honest. Imperfect. Real.

At thirteen, I had my own revelation—a personal encounter with Christ that no one could explain away. It wasn't secondhand. It was mine—not about religion or tradition, but about knowing the God who made me, loved me, and called me by name.

He said, "Do this," and I did.

I'll never forget telling my dad. His awe—torn between wonder and reverence—marked us both. How could a boy hear the Lord of Hosts, the Almighty God, so clearly? Yet the Lord had revealed Himself to his son.

As my faith grew, books like *Evidence That Demands a Verdict* by Josh McDowell and *Mere Christianity* by C.S. Lewis deepened my understanding. McDowell's work felt like a courtroom, proving Scripture's reliability and Jesus' resurrection. Lewis's book presented a logical case, demanding a choice: Liar, Lunatic, or Lord.

They stirred my mind, but my spirit sensed there was more. The Kingdom of God isn't built on arguments alone. Jesus wasn't just vindicated—He was crucified in a courtroom.

I learned that reason brings us to the threshold of belief, but only awe carries us across. Faith isn't just logical—it's beautiful, deliberate, divine.

Why This Book

That awe at Christ's voice opened my eyes to Scripture's patterns—a divine equation woven through thirty prophets, all pointing to Jesus Christ.

The Prophetic Equation is born from this: God's Word isn't just defendable; it's breathtakingly designed.

While some see Scripture as ancient stories, I see a deliberate design, rooted not in codes or theories but in a relationship with the living God.

The evidence is real. The patterns are clear. Most importantly, the Person behind it all is real—still calling us to know Him.

Welcome to the journey.

Introduction

The Bible is not a random anthology. It's not a loose collection of old stories stitched together by chance.

It is a divine masterpiece woven across centuries, cultures, empires, and languages. Yet, it speaks with a single, unified heartbeat: Jesus Christ.

Scripture reveals a breathtaking design from the opening words of Genesis to the final vision of Revelation. Every covenant, prophecy, story, and promise leads toward one Person—God's promised Redeemer. It's not chaos. It's not coincidence. It's a pattern, a plan, a person.

Among the many layers of meaning and beauty in the Bible, one aspect is often overlooked: the numbers.

Not just symbolic numbers like three, seven, or forty. But even the very counts of days, of generations, of witnesses. Even the number of prophets God raised up to speak on His behalf.

Numbers in the Bible are not ornamental. They are foundational. They are fingerprints of divine design.

Before we go any further, it's essential to make something very clear: This is not a book about numerology. It's not about mystical codes, hidden formulas, or secret messages. It's not about twisting Scripture to find patterns that God never intended.

And it's not about dry, academic number theory either.

This book is about something far simpler and far deeper: It's about recognizing the intentional patterns God has woven into His Word—patterns that highlight His character, reveal His promises, and always point to Christ.

You see, I've noticed patterns easily since I was a kid. Those logic tests where you had to find the missing piece in a sequence? I loved them. While others puzzled over shapes and numbers, the answer would almost jump off the page to me.

Later in life, I pursued a degree in mathematics, drawn to the beauty of patterns, systems, and structure. But long before I ever studied proofs and theorems, my mind was wired to recognize connections others might miss.

When I became a follower of Christ and began studying Scripture seriously, I noticed something that felt both familiar and overwhelming: God built His Word with the same careful, breathtaking intentionality.

Patterns didn't just exist—they proclaimed His glory. Numbers weren't just facts—they were fingerprints. And one of the most striking patterns I discovered was found in the prophets.

Across the pages of the Old Testament, about thirty prophets are named. Thirty distinct voices. Thirty messengers of judgment, hope, warning, and redemption.

Why thirty? Why that particular number?

Throughout Scripture, the number thirty is charged with significance. When he stood before Pharaoh, Joseph was thirty years old and stepped into his destiny. David was thirty when he became king over Israel. Jesus was thirty when He began His public ministry, fulfilling everything the Law and the Prophets pointed toward.

Thirty is the number of maturity, of readiness, of public calling.

Could it be that the thirty named prophets were not historical figures recorded at random but carefully chosen witnesses, placed like stars in the sky, pointing to one central event?

Could it be that these thirty voices, across centuries and empires, form part of a divine equation?

Could it be that their placement, their timing, their very existence speaks to a pattern bigger than any of them individually—a pattern that adds up to one answer: Jesus Christ?

That's the journey this book invites you to take.

This is not about chasing secret codes or twisting numbers to fit a theory. It is about stepping back and seeing God's breathtaking, deliberate, undeniable design.

Thirty prophets. One equation. Zero coincidence.

Together, we'll trace the pattern, examine the equation, and stand in awe of the God who wrote it—pointing, always, to His Son.

As we begin, we'll first step back and see the broader truth: In Scripture, numbers have always carried meaning, not as superstition, but as signposts of God's deliberate plan.

Before we zoom in on the thirty prophets, let's explore how numbers like three, seven, twelve, forty, and seventy have already revealed His perfect design.

Let's start at the beginning—with the patterns God built into everything.

Chapter 1

Divine Patterns: The Numbers of Scripture and God's Redemptive Plan

The Bible brims with numbers—not as curiosities or mystical codes, but as divine fingerprints.

From Genesis, God weaves His creation with number and pattern, each signaling a deeper purpose: seven days to shape the heavens and earth, twelve sons to establish the tribes of Israel, forty days of floodwaters, seventy descendants after Babel.

These are not random. They reveal divine truths, moments of completeness, and God's redemptive plan.

Faithful Bible teachers—Adrian Rogers, J. Vernon McGee, Clarence Larkin, E.W. Bullinger, and Chuck Missler—have illuminated these patterns. Chuck Missler, a former naval officer and founder of Koinonia House, a ministry dedicated to biblical study, showed how numbers point to Scripture's divine design. He taught that the Bible is an integrated message system, engineered beyond time, revealing a plan only God could orchestrate.

Not every number carries symbolic weight, but certain recurrences demand attention. What do these patterns reveal about God's design? Here are the most significant, with examples that make their meaning clear.

1 – Unity Biblical Meaning: Wholeness, oneness in God. Example: "Hear, O Israel: The Lord our God, the Lord is one" (Deuteronomy 6:4). God's unity anchors His people's oneness, as Jesus prayed: "That they may be one as we are one" (John 17:21).

2 – Witness / Testimony Biblical Meaning: Truth established through agreement. Example: Scripture requires two witnesses to confirm truth (Deuteronomy 19:15; 2 Corinthians 13:1).

Jesus sent disciples in pairs, and the Two Witnesses in Revelation testify to God's truth.

3 – Divine Perfection / The Trinity Biblical Meaning: God's fullness and completeness. Example: The triune God—Father, Son, and Holy Spirit. Jesus rose on the third day. Triads like "Holy, holy, holy" (Isaiah 6:3) reflect divine perfection.

3.5 – Tribulation / Interrupted Perfection Biblical Meaning: A season of trial, disrupting completeness. Example: Many scholars see 3.5 as symbolizing interrupted perfection (7 divided by 2). In Daniel and Revelation, 3.5 years—1,260 days or 42 months—marks the Great Tribulation, a testing period where God's protection seems withdrawn but never removed.

4 – Earth / Creation Biblical Meaning: The physical world's completeness. Example: Four directions, four winds, four rivers from Eden (Genesis 2:10-14). On the fourth day, God created the sun, moon, and stars.

5 – Grace Biblical Meaning: God's unearned favor. Example: Five offerings in Leviticus enable relationship with God. David's five stones (1 Samuel 17:40) reflect grace in battle.

6 – Man / Incompleteness Biblical Meaning: Humanity apart from God, limited. Example: Man was created on the sixth day. The number 666 (Revelation 13:18) marks the beast, mimicking divine perfection but falling short. Mathematically, 6 is a "perfect number" (its divisors sum to itself), but biblically, it warns of pride's false completeness.

7 – Completion / Spiritual Perfection Biblical Meaning: Divine fullness and rest. Example: God rested on the seventh day. Jericho fell after seven priests marched for seven days—Revelation's sevens—churches, seals, spirits—mark divine rest.

8 – New Beginning Biblical Meaning: Resurrection, rebirth. Example: Jesus rose on the eighth day, the start of a new week. Eight souls survived in Noah's ark, symbolizing new beginnings.

9 – Fruitfulness / Finality Biblical Meaning: Harvest, outcomes. Example: Nine fruits of the Spirit (Galatians 5:22-23). Jesus died at the ninth hour (Matthew 27:46), sealing His mission.

10 – Law / Responsibility Biblical Meaning: Divine order, accountability. Example: Ten Commandments, ten plagues, ten virgins in Jesus' parable. Ten reflects God's covenant standard.

11 – Disorder / Judgment Biblical Meaning: Chaos, rebellion. Example: The Tower of Babel (Genesis 11) brought confusion. Judas's betrayal left eleven disciples, marking instability before restoration, as E.W. Bullinger notes.

12 – Governmental Perfection Biblical Meaning: Divine authority. Example: Twelve tribes, twelve apostles, twelve gates in the New Jerusalem reflect God's perfect governance.

These numbers are no accident—God delights in patterns, weaving His signature across Scripture. Every number whispers His redemptive plan through Christ.

If God embeds meaning in numbers like 3, 7, and 12, might He also weave significance into His chosen messengers?

The Old Testament names roughly thirty prophets—thirty voices crying out across centuries, each pointing to God's eternal plan. Could their number, like the patterns of 7 or 12, carry divine weight? Does thirty, echoing Jesus' age at the start of His ministry, signal a completed witness?

This is the mystery we'll unfold next, revealing how God's prophets form a pattern as deliberate as the numbers themselves.

Dig Deeper: How do God's patterns in Scripture deepen your trust in His plan? What might the number 7 teach you about rest today?

Chapter 2
The Significance of Thirty

I f numbers like 3, 7, 12, 40, and 70 carry divine weight in Scripture, what about 30?

Less celebrated than 7 or 40, 30 emerges as a quiet but powerful marker of readiness, maturity, and divine calling—a threshold where hidden preparation yields to public mission.

Consider Joseph. After years of slavery and imprisonment, he stood before Pharaoh at 30, interpreting dreams and rising as a savior for nations in famine (Genesis 41:46).

Consider David. After tending sheep, slaying giants, and fleeing Saul, he was crowned king at 30, God's anointed to establish an everlasting covenant (2 Samuel 5:4).

Consider Jesus. After a life of humble obedience, He stepped into public ministry at 30, baptized by John and revealed as the Lamb of God (Luke 3:23).

Three pivotal figures. Three stories of preparation culminating at 30.

In biblical culture, 30 marked readiness. Priests began temple service at 30 (Numbers 4:3), the age of spiritual accountability, poised to bear sacred responsibilities.

This pattern of commissioning at 30 connects to the roughly 30 prophets named in the Old Testament—voices like Isaiah, Jeremiah, Ezekiel, Hosea, Amos, Elijah, and Samuel. While figures such as Moses or Deborah prophesied, they're often classified as lawgivers or judges rather than prophets in the narrower sense, keeping the count near 30.

These 30 prophets weren't scattered by chance. Each, like Joseph, David, and Jesus, emerged at God's appointed time to warn, comfort, or reveal the coming King.

Together, they form a divine chorus—30 signposts on the road to redemption, each voice a thread in God's redemptive tapestry.

This is the heart of this book: God's patterns—in numbers, people, and history—point to Christ. The 30 prophets are no coincidence but part of a divine equation, each contributing to the revelation of the Messiah.

The number is intentional. The plan is perfect. The Savior is no accident.

Next, we'll explore how these 30 voices weave together, each adding a unique note to the symphony of God's unfolding plan.

Dig Deeper: How does the pattern of 30 inspire you to trust God's timing in your own calling?

Chapter 3
The Equation

If you've ever tackled a math equation, you know the principle: some parts are constants—fixed values that never waver. Others are variables—factors that shift with the situation. Yet when the equation is properly set up, all the pieces converge to one clear solution.

The Bible's prophetic story works the same way:

Constants + Variables = One Solution

Across history, God's constants remain unshakable: His holiness, His covenant promises, His plan for redemption. The variables—the prophets themselves—enter at different times, in different places, speaking into unique moments of crisis or hope. Yet the outcome is always the same: the equation resolves to one answer—Jesus Christ.

Let's break this down.

The Constants

Certain truths anchor God's story of redemption, unchanging through time or culture:

- **God's Character:** He is holy, just, merciful, and faithful—unchanging from eternity past to eternity future.

- **God's Covenant:** His binding promises, like those to Abraham (Genesis 12:1-3) to bless all nations and to David (2 Samuel 7:12-16) for an everlasting kingdom, stand firm.

- **God's Mission:** He is committed to rescuing humanity from sin and restoring all things through His Messiah, the promised Savior.

These constants are the bedrock of every prophecy and promise, from the Garden of Eden to the cross of Calvary.

The Variables

The prophets are the variables, each unique in their context and calling:

They appear across centuries, from Moses in Egypt to Malachi in the post-exile era. They speak to different audiences: Isaiah advised kings, while Amos, a humble farmer, confronted injustice. Their messages vary: Ezekiel's visions warned of judgment, while Hosea's life embodied God's tender mercy.

Some were priests. Some were shepherds. Some delivered fiery rebukes; others offered hope. Their methods, audiences, and stories differ, yet each prophet moves the equation forward, adding revelation, confirming promises, and sharpening the picture of the Messiah to come.

One Solution: Christ

In a mathematical equation, constants and variables resolve to a single answer. In God's story, every prophetic voice—through exile and return, judgment and mercy—points to one solution.

Not a theory. Not a philosophy. Not a new religion.

A Person.

Jesus Christ.

He is the fulfillment of every prophetic whisper, the realization of every covenant promise, the Savior the prophets yearned for, even when they saw only glimpses of the full picture. As Paul writes in 2 Corinthians 1:20, "For every one of God's promises is 'Yes' in Him."

Every variable converges in Him. Every pattern resolves in Him. While some might view these prophecies as merely historical or cultural, Christians see them as divine pointers to Christ, the One who embodies God's plan.

The Divine Equation

This is the equation:

Constants (God's unchanging nature) + Variables (thirty prophetic voices) = One Solution (Jesus).

Why thirty prophets? Across Scripture, from Moses to Malachi, thirty distinct voices—major prophets like Isaiah and minor prophets like Micah, as well as others without books—form a complete tapestry of revelation. Their diversity underscores the richness of God's plan, yet their unity confirms its precision.

In the chapters ahead, we'll explore these voices—major prophets thundering in royal courts, minor prophets crying out in obscure towns, and silent prophets whose lives spoke louder than words. Each one adds a piece to this divine equation.

Step back, and you'll see it: this is no random collection of stories. It's not chaos.

It's a masterpiece of divine mathematics.

And it all adds up to Jesus.

Come see how every line points to the One who completes the story.

Chapter 4
Major Prophets, Major Clues

I f the prophets form a divine equation, the Major Prophets are its loudest voices—bold, expansive, and foundational.

Their title doesn't imply greater importance, only longer writings, sweeping across judgment, restoration, and future glory. Isaiah, Jeremiah, Ezekiel, and Daniel anchor the Old Testament's prophetic witness, their voices uniting to proclaim God's promised Messiah, the Savior.

Each spoke at a distinct time, with unique burdens and visions. Yet together, they offer breathtaking glimpses of Jesus Christ. While some view their words as merely historical, Christians see them as divine pointers to Him.

They are key variables in the equation that resolve in Jesus.

Let's meet them.

Isaiah: The Voice of Salvation

Isaiah's name, meaning "The Lord is salvation," echoes through his book like a river. He paints a vivid portrait of the Messiah, God's promised Savior.

A virgin will conceive a son called Immanuel (Isaiah 7:14). A suffering servant will be pierced for our sins (Isaiah 53). A descendant of David will rule in righteousness (Isaiah 9:6-7).

Jesus quoted Isaiah to define His mission (Luke 4:17-21), showing these visions found their fulfillment in Him.

Isaiah sees humanity's brokenness and the beauty of redemption—a Savior who comes not in splendor, but in humility and sacrifice.

In the divine equation, Isaiah adds: The Messiah will be both suffering servant and reigning King.

Jeremiah: The Voice of the New Covenant

Known as the "weeping prophet," Jeremiah grieved Jerusalem's fall and God's people's exile to Babylon. Yet amid sorrow, he delivered a transformative promise: a new covenant, a divine promise of heart-level change.

"I will put My law within them and write it on their hearts. I will be their God, and they shall be My people" (Jeremiah 31:33).

Not stone tablets, but hearts renewed. Jesus echoed this at the Last Supper (Luke 22:20), fulfilling Jeremiah's vision.

In the divine equation, Jeremiah adds: The Messiah will forge a heart-level covenant.

Ezekiel: The Voice of Resurrection

Exiled in Babylon after Jerusalem's fall, Ezekiel spoke to a people stripped of hope. His visions—wheels within wheels, dry bones rattling to life, a renewed temple—pulse with divine power.

In Ezekiel 37, a valley of dry bones comes to life as a living army, a symbol of resurrection. God promises not just a return from exile, but a renewal of hearts and nations. Jesus fulfilled this, declaring, "I am the resurrection and the life" (John 11:25).

In the divine equation, Ezekiel adds: The Messiah will bring resurrection and restoration.

Daniel: The Voice of Sovereignty

In Babylon's pagan courts, Daniel stood faithful. His visions of rising and falling empires revealed a greater truth: a "Son of Man" coming with clouds, receiving eternal dominion (Daniel 7:13-14).

Jesus claimed this title (Mark 14:61-62), showing He is the King whose Kingdom outlasts all others.

In the divine equation, Daniel adds: The Messiah is the sovereign Son of Man, ruling an eternal Kingdom.

A Unified Witness

Why these four? Their expansive books weave a panoramic view of God's plan—judgment, exile, and restoration. Together, they form a composite:

Isaiah: A Savior who suffers and reigns. Jeremiah: A covenant that transforms hearts. Ezekiel: A restoration beyond death. Daniel: A Kingdom that never ends.

Not scattered voices, but coordinated witnesses. Jesus quoted each, showing He fulfills their words.

Thirty prophets. One equation. Zero coincidence.

Next, we'll explore the Minor Prophets—smaller books, but voices no less vital in pointing to the One who completes the story.

Chapter 5
The Minor Prophets Speak Loudly

The Major Prophets spoke with sweeping visions. The Minor Prophets, by contrast, deliver compact intensity—brief messages packed with power, like small variables carrying enormous weight in the divine equation.

"Minor" refers to their books' length, not their impact. Their voices are anything but small.

Twelve voices. Twelve messengers. Twelve pieces of the divine puzzle.

Each brings a glimpse, warning, promise, or hope—forming a chorus pointing to Jesus Christ, the Messiah. While some view their words as historical warnings, Christians hear them proclaiming the Savior.

Let's hear their voices.

Hosea: Love That Redeems

Hosea, speaking to Israel before it fell to Assyria, lived a prophecy. His marriage to an unfaithful wife mirrored Israel's betrayal of God. Yet his relentless love reflects Christ, the faithful Bridegroom, redeeming His Church at great cost.

Joel: Spirit Outpoured

Joel, prophesying during a time of crisis, foretold the Day of the Lord—a time of divine judgment and renewal—and God's Spirit poured out on all. Peter quoted Joel at Pentecost (Acts 2:16-21), showing Christ fulfills this promise.

Amos: Justice and Righteousness

Amos, a shepherd in Judah's moral decline, thundered against injustice. He called for righteousness like a mighty river. Jesus embodies perfect justice, flooding the earth with true righteousness.

Obadiah: Victory Over Pride

Obadiah, addressing Edom's pride before its fall, warned that proud kingdoms crumble before God's King. In Christ, pride is defeated, and humble faith reigns in His eternal Kingdom.

Jonah: Death, Burial, and Resurrection

Jonah, sent to Nineveh, was swallowed by a great fish for three days, emerging to preach mercy. Jesus pointed to Jonah as a sign of His death, burial, and resurrection (Matthew 12:40).

Micah: The Birthplace of the Messiah

Micah, prophesying during Judah's decline, pinpointed Bethlehem as the Messiah's birthplace: "From you shall come forth...one who is to be ruler" (Micah 5:2). Jesus' birth fulfilled this divine design.

Nahum: The God Who Judges

Nahum, proclaiming Nineveh's doom, thundered God's certain justice. His words foreshadow Christ's return to judge evil and establish His righteous rule.

Habakkuk: Faith That Saves

Habakkuk, wrestling with evil in Judah's dark days, declared, "The righteous shall live by faith" (Habakkuk 2:4). This truth, echoed in Romans 1:17, is fulfilled in Christ's gospel.

Zephaniah: Rejoicing Over the Redeemed

Zephaniah warned of judgment but sang of God rejoicing over His people with love. Through Christ, God's people are restored to joyful communion.

Haggai: The True Temple

Haggai, urging the exiles to rebuild the temple, pointed to a greater reality. Jesus, the true temple, was destroyed and raised in three days (John 2:19).

Zechariah: The Coming King

Zechariah, in post-exile Judah, saw a king on a donkey, a struck shepherd, a pierced Savior. Every vision points to Jesus' final week.

Malachi: Preparing the Way

Malachi, closing the Old Testament, promised a messenger to prepare the way for the Lord. John the Baptist fulfilled this, heralding Christ.

One Major Message

The Minor Prophets form a unified testimony:

- Hosea: A faithful Redeemer.

- Joel: An outpoured Spirit.

- Amos: Justice and righteousness.

- Obadiah: Victory over pride.

- Jonah: Death and resurrection.

- Micah: A Messiah from Bethlehem.

- Nahum: Certain judgment.

- Habakkuk: Salvation by faith.

- Zephaniah: Joyful restoration.

- Haggai: The true temple.

- Zechariah: A coming King.

- Malachi: A prepared way.

Different voices. Different times. One Savior: Jesus.

Thirty prophets. One equation. Zero coincidence.

Next, meet the prophets without books—lives and words that still point to the One who completes the story.

Chapter 6
The Prophets Without Books

Not every prophet in the Bible left behind a scroll etched with their name. Some blazed through history like wildfire—speaking bold truths, anointing kings, calling down fire, or whispering hope in moments of despair.

Their voices, though unwritten, echo across centuries, each adding a vital piece to the divine equation of God's redemptive plan. These prophets without books stood at the crossroads of Israel's story, confronting sin, renewing covenant hope, and pointing unerringly to the coming of Christ.

Let's meet them, feel the weight of their moments, and see how their lives weave into the pattern of the Messiah.

Samuel: The Kingmaker Who Heard God's Whisper

Samuel's story begins in the quiet of a barren woman's prayer and ends as a towering legacy in Israel's history. Born to Hannah, a woman of fervent faith, he grew up in the tabernacle, learning to hear God's voice in a time when it was rare (1 Samuel 3:1).

As the last judge and first great prophet, Samuel bridged eras, anointing Israel's first two kings: Saul, the flawed warrior, and David, the shepherd whose heart beat for God.

In anointing David, Samuel set in motion God's covenant plan. From David's line would come the Messiah—the true King, whose reign would know no end.

Picture Samuel, oil in hand, standing before a young shepherd, seeing not just a boy but the lineage of salvation. His life whispers to us: the Messiah would be the eternal King from David's house, fulfilling God's promise to a broken nation.

Nathan: The Covenant Messenger Who Spoke Truth to Power

Nathan stood before kings, unafraid to wield God's truth like a sword. When David fell into sin with Bathsheba, Nathan's parable of the stolen lamb pierced the king's heart, leading to repentance (2 Samuel 12:1-14).

But Nathan's role extended beyond rebuke. He delivered God's unbreakable promise: David's throne would endure forever (2 Samuel 7:16). This covenant wasn't just about a dynasty; it was a divine blueprint for the Messiah, the Son of David, whose kingdom would be eternal.

Imagine Nathan's courage, standing before a king to deliver both judgment and hope. His words shaped history, pointing to Jesus, the King who would rule with justice and mercy. Nathan's life adds to the equation: the Messiah would fulfill an everlasting covenant, transforming a throne of wood into a throne of glory.

Elijah: The Fire-Bearer Who Challenged a Nation

Elijah burst onto the scene like a thunderclap, confronting King Ahab and the prophets of Baal in a nation drunk on idolatry.

On Mount Carmel, he stood alone, calling fire from heaven to consume a water-soaked altar (1 Kings 18:36-39). The flames didn't just burn wood; they burned away doubt, proving Yahweh alone is God.

Elijah's life was a battle cry against false worship, calling Israel back to its true King.

Centuries later, Elijah stood beside Jesus at the Transfiguration (Matthew 17:3), his presence testifying that Christ was the fulfillment of all prophecy.

Elijah's ministry shouts to us: the Messiah would confront falsehood, restore true worship, and wield divine power to reveal God's glory.

Elisha: The Miracle-Worker Who Foreshadowed Life

Elisha, Elijah's successor, carried a double portion of his mentor's spirit and a mantle of miracles.

He purified poisoned water (2 Kings 2:19-22), multiplied oil for a desperate widow (2 Kings 4:1-7), and raised a dead boy to life (2 Kings 4:32-35). Each act was a glimpse of God's compassion, a foretaste of the One who would come.

Imagine the widow's tears as oil overflowed, or a mother's joy as her son breathed again—these were shadows of Christ's greater works.

Jesus would heal the sick, feed thousands, and raise the dead, fulfilling Elisha's miracles on a cosmic scale.

Elisha's life sings to us: the Messiah would bring healing, provision, and resurrection, turning despair into hope.

Gad: The Counselor Who Guided Repentance

Gad, a prophet in David's court, spoke truth when it was hardest to hear.

After David's sinful census, Gad delivered God's judgment but also offered a path to restoration (2 Samuel 24:11-19).

Picture Gad standing before a humbled king, guiding him to build an altar where mercy would prevail. His role was not just to correct but to restore, pointing David—and Israel—back to God.

Gad's ministry reminds us that the Messiah would be more than a Savior; He would be the Prophet calling all to repentance, offering forgiveness to those who turn to Him.

Huldah: The Prophetess Who Sparked Renewal

In a time of spiritual decay, Huldah emerged as a beacon of God's truth.

When King Josiah rediscovered the Book of the Law, he sought Huldah's counsel (2 Kings 22:14-20). Her words confirmed God's judgment but also His mercy for a repentant king.

Imagine Huldah, a woman of wisdom, speaking with authority to a nation on the brink of revival. Her prophecy fueled Josiah's reforms, turning Israel back to its covenant roots.

Huldah's life declares: the Messiah would fulfill the Law and the Prophets, calling God's people to renewal and restoring their covenant with Him.

Prophets Without Books, Voices Without Gaps

These prophets left no scrolls, but their lives wrote volumes in the story of redemption:

Samuel anointed the royal line, setting the stage for the King of Kings. Nathan delivered the covenant that promised an eternal throne. Elijah confronted idolatry, standing with Christ as a witness to His divinity. Elisha's miracles foreshadowed the life-giving power of Jesus. Gad guided repentance, pointing to the Messiah's call for transformed hearts. Huldah sparked renewal, echoing Christ's mission to restore God's covenant.

Different lives. Different eras. One mission.

Each prophet, like a brushstroke on a divine canvas, added to the portrait of the Messiah.

Their stories, woven across centuries, form an equation with no variables left to chance.

Thirty prophets. One Christ. Zero coincidence.

In the next chapter, we'll step back to see the larger patterns woven through these prophetic lives—the recurring numbers, the shared themes, and the unmistakable echoes that all point forward to Christ. From cycles of judgment and mercy to the sacred symbolism of numbers, each thread adds clarity to the divine equation.

Chapter 7

Patterns in the Prophets

Patterns in the Prophets

Step back and gaze across the tapestry of the thirty prophets, and something breathtaking emerges: patterns, woven like golden threads through their lives, words, and warnings.

These are not random voices crying in the wilderness; they are notes in a divine symphony, each resonating with the others, harmonizing across centuries to sing one song—redemption through the coming Christ.

The numbers they spoke, the themes they echoed, the stories they lived—all interlock with precision, forming an equation too deliberate to be chance.

Let's trace these patterns and see how they point, unerringly, to Jesus, the heart of God's plan.

The Numbers That Pulse with Purpose

In Scripture, numbers are more than markers; they are signposts of God's design, pulsing through the prophets' messages like a heartbeat.

These recurring figures—three, seven, forty, seventy—carry divine weight, each tying the prophets' words to the Messiah's mission.

Three: Divine Completeness

Picture Jonah, swallowed by the deep, entombed in a fish's belly for three days (Jonah 1:17). Then see Jesus, buried in the earth, rising on the third day (Matthew 12:40).

Three marks moments of divine fulfillment—Hosea's promise of restoration "after two days, on the third day" (Hosea 6:2) finds its echo in Christ's resurrection, the ultimate completion of God's plan.

Every prophetic "three" whispers: the Messiah will bring life from death.

Seven: Perfection and Rest

Jeremiah foretold seventy years of captivity (Jeremiah 25:11), a perfect cycle of sabbaths leading to restoration. Zechariah's visions of seven lamps (Zechariah 4:2) evoke God's perfect Spirit, illuminating His people.

Jesus, resting in the tomb on the seventh day, fulfilled the Sabbath, offering eternal rest (Hebrews 4:9-10).

Seven signs of God's perfect timing, and the prophets' sevens point to Christ, the perfection of God's promise.

Forty: Testing and Transformation

Imagine Elijah, fleeing to Horeb, fasting forty days in the wilderness (1 Kings 19:8), or Israel, wandering forty years to learn dependence (Numbers 14:33-34).

Jesus, fasting forty days before His ministry (Matthew 4:2), stepped into this pattern, facing temptation and emerging victorious.

Every prophetic forty—whether Moses on Sinai or Ezekiel's days of bearing sin (Ezekiel 4:6)—prepares the way for the Messiah, who transforms testing into triumph.

Seventy: Nations, Judgment, Mercy

Jeremiah's seventy years of exile (Jeremiah 29:10) promised both judgment and mercy, a restoration for God's people. Daniel's seventy weeks (Daniel 9:24) mapped the path to the Messiah's arrival.

Jesus sent out seventy disciples (Luke 10:1; some manuscripts read seventy-two), extending mercy to all nations.

Each prophetic seventy reminds us: Christ will judge sin, show mercy, and gather all people to Himself.

These numbers aren't accidents. They are the rhythm of God's covenant, pulsing through the prophets' voices, counting down to the One who fulfills them all.

The Themes That Bind the Prophets' Hearts

Beyond numbers, the prophets share themes that weave their ministries into a single story.

These threads—wilderness, judgment and mercy, exile and return, covenant and restoration—run through their words like rivers, converging in the person of Christ.

Wilderness and Testing

The wilderness is more than a place; it's a crucible.

Israel wandered forty years, tested and refined (Deuteronomy 8:2). Elijah fled to the wilderness, sustained by God's provision (1 Kings

19:4-8). John the Baptist cried out from the desert, "Prepare the way!" (Matthew 3:3).

Jesus entered the wilderness, fasting forty days and defeating Satan (Matthew 4:1-11), succeeding where Israel faltered.

The prophets' wilderness stories proclaim: the Messiah will endure testing, leading us to new life.

Judgment and Mercy

Picture Amos, thundering against Israel's injustice (Amos 5:24), or Isaiah, warning of coming judgment yet promising a Suffering Servant (Isaiah 53).

Every prophet carried this dual message: God's fierce love demands justice but delights in mercy.

Jesus fulfilled this rhythm, bearing the judgment of sin on the cross so mercy could flow freely (Romans 3:25-26).

The prophets' warnings and promises find their answer in Him—the One who judges rightly and restores completely.

Exile and Return

Jeremiah wept over Judah's exile (Jeremiah 9:1), yet foresaw a return (Jeremiah 32:37). Ezekiel envisioned dry bones living again (Ezekiel 37). Haggai and Zechariah spurred the exiles to rebuild.

But exile's true end wasn't a city or temple; it was Christ, who ends our spiritual exile from God (Ephesians 2:13-14).

The prophets' cries for homecoming echo in Jesus, the way back to the Father.

Covenant and Restoration

From Moses to Malachi, the prophets upheld God's covenant, even when Israel strayed.

Jeremiah's new covenant (Jeremiah 31:31-34)—written on hearts, not stone—found its fulfillment in Christ's blood (Hebrews 9:15).

Isaiah's vision of a renewed creation (Isaiah 65:17) points to Jesus, who makes all things new (Revelation 21:5).

The prophets' promises of restoration converge in the Messiah, the covenant's perfect keeper.

A Symphony Too Precise to Ignore

Thirty prophets, spanning centuries, kingdoms, and crises. Yet their voices blend into a single melody.

Their numbers—three, seven, forty, seventy—pulse with divine intent.

Their themes—wilderness, judgment, exile, covenant—interweave like chords, each resolving in Christ.

This is no coincidence; it's a composition, written by the hand of God.

Imagine the prophets as stars in a constellation, each shining in its place, yet together forming the outline of a Savior.

Their patterns point not to a vague hope but to a living Person—Jesus Christ, the sum of every prophetic word, the answer to every divine equation.

Thirty prophets. One Christ. Zero coincidence.

In the next chapter, we'll explore how time itself becomes a prophetic variable, stretching across centuries but never straying from the path to Christ.

Chapter 8
Time as a Prophetic Variable

I n any equation, variables shift, but if the constants hold, the solution endures.

One of the most remarkable variables in the prophetic equation is time. The thirty prophets we've been studying spanned centuries of history. Different kings. Different kingdoms. Different threats. Different cultures.

Yet, across these vast stretches, their voices harmonized. Their messages aligned. Their warnings, promises, and visions wove into a single pattern—one that finds its ultimate resolution in Jesus Christ.

Time didn't unravel the equation. It revealed its truth.

Prophets Across the Centuries

Picture the timeline:

Samuel (ca. 1100 BC) anointed Israel's first kings amidst tribal turmoil. Isaiah (700s BC) spoke as Assyria threatened Judah's survival. Jeremiah (600s-500s BC) mourned Jerusalem's fall to Babylon. Ezekiel and Daniel (500s BC) offered hope from Babylonian exile. Haggai, Zechariah, and Malachi (500s-400s BC) urged perseverance during Jerusalem's restoration.

These prophets spanned over 600 years—a period as distant as our time from the age of Columbus. Languages shifted. Empires rose and crumbled. Cultures transformed beyond recognition.

Yet, the prophetic message remained unshakably consistent:

A Messiah will come. He will redeem God's people. He will suffer, yet reign. He will bring justice and mercy. He will establish an everlasting Kingdom.

Different eras. Same constants. Same Savior.

Prophecies Layered Through Time

Prophecies often served dual purposes: addressing immediate crises while pointing to a distant future. This layered design reveals God's precision and underscores why early Christians could confidently demonstrate Jesus as the long-promised Messiah.

Consider Isaiah 7:14:

"The Lord himself will give you a sign: The virgin will conceive and give birth to a son, and will call him Immanuel."

In its immediate context, this reassured King Ahaz of God's presence during a political crisis, likely pointing to a child born in his era (Isaiah 8:3-4). Yet, Matthew 1:22-23 unveils its ultimate fulfillment in Jesus' virgin birth—a divine sign transcending time.

Similarly, Daniel 7:13-14 envisions "one like a son of man" receiving eternal dominion. For exiles in Babylon, this promised God's triumph over oppressive empires like Persia, Greece, and Rome, foretold in Daniel's visions (Daniel 2, Daniel 7). Jesus later claims this title (Mark 14:62), fulfilling it in His first coming and pointing to His eternal reign at His return.

Micah 5:2 declares:

"But you, Bethlehem Ephrathah, though you are small among the clans of Judah, out of you will come for me one who will be ruler over Israel."

In Micah's day, this bolstered Judah's hope, promising a Davidic leader from an obscure village. Centuries later, it precisely pinpointed Jesus' birthplace (Matthew 2:5-6), defying human odds.

Skeptics might call these coincidences, but the precision across centuries—spanning cultures, languages, and empires points to a divine mind weaving history toward one purpose. These weren't vague predictions. They were promises, layered across time, fulfilling immediate needs while building toward ultimate redemption.

Preserving the Prophetic Word

How did these prophecies endure across centuries?

Scribes meticulously recorded them on scrolls, with later groups like the Masoretes ensuring every letter was preserved with astonishing accuracy. Oral traditions, rooted in Israel's covenantal worship, reinforced their fidelity before written records solidified.

Centuries before Christ, the Hebrew Scriptures were translated into Greek (the Septuagint), spreading these prophecies across the Mediterranean world.

Synagogues and early Christian communities guarded these texts as sacred, even through invasions and exiles. The discovery of the Dead Sea Scrolls, nearly identical to later manuscripts, confirms this remarkable preservation.

Through God's providence, the prophetic word stood firm, its message undimmed by time.

The Variable of Time—and the Constant Faithfulness of God

The centuries-long sweep of prophecy makes its consistency breathtaking. Only a sovereign God could orchestrate:

Dozens of prophets, across countless generations, under shifting rulers and regimes, in diverse cities, languages, and landscapes, all pointing to one unified hope.

Time didn't weaken the message. It amplified its power.

In mathematics, a variable may change, but a true equation yields the same solution. In Scripture, time is the ultimate variable. And the solution remains Christ.

Time Was Never the Enemy

The gap between prophecy and fulfillment wasn't a flaw—it was intentional. The delay tested faith, refined hope, and revealed God's patience.

As Galatians 4:4 declares:

"When the fullness of time had come, God sent forth His Son."

God wasn't slow. He wasn't late. He was perfectly on time.

Each prophet built on those before, layering promise upon promise, until the cornerstone Himself appeared.

Thirty prophets. One equation. No coincidence.

Next, we'll trace how Jesus fulfilled these ancient promises, proving the equation wasn't just elegant—it was eternal.

Chapter 9
Fulfilled and Final

An equation isn't solved until the answer is proven. Prophecies aren't fulfilled until the promises are kept.

Across centuries, thirty prophets laid down pieces of the equation—hints, glimpses, declarations, and dreams. Some immediate. Some distant. Some so precise they seemed impossible.

Then Jesus came. Not merely claiming to fulfill prophecy, but embodying it—openly, specifically, completely. Every piece of the prophetic pattern found its yes in Him.

Fulfillment in His Birth

From His first breath, Jesus fulfilled ancient promises:

Born of a virgin (Isaiah 7:14)—Mary's miraculous conception defied nature. Born in Bethlehem (Micah 5:2)—a small village, not Jerusalem, as foretold. Called out of Egypt (Hosea 11:1)—fulfilled when Joseph and Mary returned with Jesus after fleeing Herod (Matthew 2:15). Descendant of David (Jeremiah 23:5)—confirmed through His lineage (Matthew 1:1).

No human could orchestrate these details. Mary and Joseph didn't manipulate empires to align with scrolls. They walked in a divine plan, step by step.

Fulfillment in His Life

His birth set the stage, and Jesus' ministry unfolded as the prophets envisioned:

A voice crying in the wilderness (Isaiah 40:3)—John the Baptist prepared His way (Matthew 3:3). Miracles of healing (Isaiah 35:5-6)—the blind saw, the deaf heard, the lame walked. Entry on a donkey (Zechariah

9:9)—Jesus rode into Jerusalem humbly, as crowds cheered (Matthew 21:5).

From birth to public life, Jesus didn't "check boxes." He lived the prophetic pattern because He was the promised One.

Fulfillment in His Death

The suffering Savior's prophecies are vivid and precise:

Betrayed by a friend (Psalm 41:9)—Judas' kiss marked the arrest. Sold for thirty pieces of silver (Zechariah 11:12-13)—Judas betrayed Jesus for this exact price, later returning the coins in guilt (Matthew 27:3-5). Silent before accusers (Isaiah 53:7)—Jesus spoke not a word in His trials. Pierced hands and feet (Psalm 22:16)—crucifixion fulfilled this centuries before its invention. Lots cast for His clothing (Psalm 22:18)—soldiers gambled at the cross. Numbered among transgressors (Isaiah 53:12)—crucified between thieves.

The cross wasn't a detour. It was the destination, etched in history with undeniable detail.

Fulfillment in His Resurrection

Jesus' victory over death confirmed the prophets' words:

Risen after three days (Hosea 6:2)—echoing Israel's hope of Messianic restoration, Jesus rose (Matthew 28:6). Sign of Jonah (Jonah 1:17)—three days in the fish prefigured His tomb (Matthew 12:40). Not abandoned to death (Psalm 16:10)—God raised Him, defying decay.

The resurrection wasn't just a miracle. It was the divine seal, proclaiming: The equation is complete. The Savior has come.

Fulfillment in His Ascension and Reign

From death to glory, Jesus' exaltation fulfills prophecy:

Seated at God's right hand (Psalm 110:1)—He reigns as Lord (Acts 2:34-35). Pouring out the

Spirit (Joel 2:28)—Peter declared this fulfilled at Pentecost, when the Spirit empowered the church (Acts 2:16-17). Coming again in glory (Daniel 7:13-14)—His return will complete His eternal reign.

The prophetic equation isn't a closed event—it's a living reality, unfolding in Christ's reign and return, assuring believers today.

No Loose Threads

Scholars estimate Jesus fulfilled over 300 distinct prophecies, from His birthplace to His betrayal. Skeptics might claim chance, but the odds of one man fulfilling dozens of precise prophecies—virgin birth, Bethlehem, thirty pieces of silver—are less than one in a trillion, scholars calculate.

If the prophets were wrong, contradictions would unravel the pattern. If Jesus were merely a teacher, the fulfillments would falter.

Yet, no thread is loose. Every promise was fulfilled.

The constants held. The variables moved. The solution emerged: Jesus.

Thirty prophets. One equation. Zero coincidence.

In our final chapter, we'll weave every prophetic voice, pattern, and promise into the singular truth of Christ—the eternal solution to God's redemptive equation.

Chapter 10
Jesus: The Sum of All Prophecy

E quations don't just need solutions. They need meaning.

The thirty prophets weren't merely solving a problem. They were revealing a Person.

Every vision, warning, promise, shadow, and glimpse points to Jesus. He is not just the One who fulfills prophecy. He is the One every prophecy exists to reveal. He is the heartbeat behind the patterns, the fulfillment of the promises, the Word behind the words. The prophets didn't just predict Christ. They proclaimed Him.

Jesus the Prophet

Jesus speaks God's perfect truth, the promised Messenger like Moses (Deuteronomy 18:15; Acts 3:22).

Jesus the Priest

He bridges the gap between God and humanity, offering Himself as the perfect sacrifice (Hebrews 7:27).

Jesus the King

He rules with justice and mercy, the King of kings over all creation (Revelation 19:16).

Jesus fulfills all three perfectly, embodying the thirty prophets' collective witness: truth declared, atonement secured, and reign established.

Jesus: The Center of All Time

From prophets to fulfillment, time itself pivots on Christ. History divides at His arrival: Before Christ (B.C.) and Anno Domini ("In the year of our Lord," A.D.). The thirty prophets' voices, spanning centuries, converged on this divine destination: Jesus.

Jesus: The Convergence of Every Pattern

Step back, and the prophetic landscape overwhelms:

The numbers align. The themes repeat. The messages converge.

Thirty prophets. One *equation*. Zero coincidence.

At the center stands Christ—not an accident, not a footnote, but the story:

- Isaiah's suffering Servant (Isaiah 53:5)

- Jeremiah's righteous Branch (Jeremiah 23:5)

- Daniel's Son of Man (Daniel 7:13)

- Hosea's faithful Husband (Hosea 2:19-20)

- Amos's perfect Judge (Amos 5:24)

- Zechariah's Shepherd (Zechariah 13:7)

- Malachi's Sun of Righteousness (Malachi 4:2)

All patterns, all voices, all hopes find their "yes" in Him (2 Corinthians 1:20).

It All Adds Up to Jesus

The Bible is no random anthology. It's a divine masterpiece. Trace the thirty prophets, their numbers, patterns, and promises, and you find not chaos, but Christ.

He is the culmination of prophecy, fulfilling every word, and the beginning of God's ongoing revelation, inviting us to trust Him today. The equation is not ancient history alone—it is alive, still summoning hearts to recognize the One it reveals.

Thirty prophets. One *equation*. Zero coincidence.

It all adds up to Jesus. It always has. It always will.

About the Author

  hristian A. Dickinson is a teacher, coach, and author who believes the Bible is not a random anthology, but a divine masterpiece — intentionally designed to point to Jesus Christ.

With a background in mathematics, engineering, leadership, education, and biblical study, he writes to help readers recognize the deliberate patterns God has woven into His Word.

His passion is simple: to magnify Christ, strengthen faith, and inspire awe for the brilliance of God's design.

Christian is the founder of Learning Engineered Publishing, where he creates faith-based devotionals, Bible studies, and Christ-centered children's literature alongside his wife, Morgan.

They live with their growing family, seeking to build a Christ-centered home rooted in faith, joy, and purpose.

Chapter 11
More by Christian A. Dickinson

If you enjoyed *The Prophetic Equation*, you may also appreciate these Christ-centered resources:

Jesus Was Funnier Than You Think: Unlocking His Wit, Wisdom, and Unexpected Humor. A fresh look at the wit and humor of Jesus Christ — revealing the brilliant, joyful ways He taught truth and disarmed pride.

Every Tear Remembered: God's Presence in Our Grief A reflection on sorrow, healing, and hope through the lens of God's enduring love.

The Curse of Time: Time Began When Eternity Broke A theological and personal exploration of time as a consequence of sin, not a neutral part of creation. Drawing from Scripture, Church Fathers, and moments of divine encounter, this book challenges the assumption that time was God's original design and invites readers to rediscover the eternal now of God's presence.

Roar of 'Ēzer: Reclaiming God's Vision for Women's Strength From Eden's garden to the early church, God named women *'ēzer*—rescuer, strength-bearer, equal partner in His image. This compelling biblical exploration invites women to rise, not as shadows but as co-laborers in God's kingdom. With Scripture, story, and a call to courage, *Roar of 'Ēzer* reveals that women were never meant to shrink. They were always meant to roar.

Micah 6:8: A Prophetic Bridge to Jesus A concise biblical commentary exploring how one ancient verse points forward to the life and ministry of Christ.

It's All or Nothing: How Jesus Raised the Standard from Tithing to Full Surrender—a biblical commentary challenging traditional views of tithing by exploring Jesus' call to radical, Spirit-led generosity.

FULL CIRCLE: PREGAME — A Devotional Series for Athletes Before the whistle blows and the lights come up, PREGAME challenges athletes to prepare their hearts as well as their bodies. With powerful stories, Scripture reflections, and real talk from the locker room, Coach Dickinson and Anthony "Diso" Paradiso equip competitors to lead with faith, play with integrity, and honor Christ in every moment.

www.ingramcontent.com/pod-product-compliance
Lightning Source LLC
Chambersburg PA
CBHW031229120626
46545CB00003B/1054